CHRISTMAS GIFTS
That Won't Break

AN ADVENT STUDY FOR ADULTS

CHRISTMAS GIFTS
That Won't Break

AN ADVENT STUDY FOR ADULTS

James W. Moore

ABINGDON PRESS
NASHVILLE

Rev. Tom Tate – 2014

CHRISTMAS GIFTS THAT WON'T BREAK
AN ADVENT STUDY FOR ADULTS

This book is printed on acid-free paper.

Library of Congress Cataloging-in-Publication Data

Moore, James W. (James Wendell), 1938–
  Christmas gifts that won't break: an Advent study for adults / James W. Moore.
    p.   cm.
  ISBN 978-1-4267-0805-3 (binding: printed/text plus-cover, adhesive-perfect binding: alk. paper)
  1. Advent—Meditations.   I. Title.
  BV40.M638   2010
  242'.332—dc22

                                                                          2010016107

All scripture quotations are taken from the New Revised Standard Version of the Bible, copyright 1989, Division of Christian Education of the National Council of the Churches of Christ in the United States of America. Used by permission. All rights reserved.

10 11 12 13 14 15 16 17 18 19—10 9 8 7 6 5 4 3 2 1

MANUFACTURED IN THE UNITED STATES OF AMERICA

Contents

✳

Introduction

Bishop Kenneth Shamblin once told a story about something that happened to his son, Ken Jr., on Christmas afternoon. Ken Jr. was about five years old at the time, and more than anything he wanted a red toy truck for Christmas that year. That's all he could talk about. He told his parents. He pointed it out to them at the toy store. He showed them a picture of it in the catalogue. He wrote to Santa. He went to the mall to tell Santa in person how much he wanted that particular red toy truck for Christmas. He even prayed about it.

Then, on Christmas morning, there it was under the tree. Ken Jr. was overjoyed! He received many other presents, but he hardly noticed them. All of his five-year-old attention was riveted on that bright, shiny, new red toy truck. For so long he had dreamed about it, and now his dream was reality.

All morning long he played with it. But then, shortly after Christmas dinner, Bishop Shamblin had just sat down in the den to read the newspaper when he heard his son crying. He laid the paper aside, and there was Ken Jr. standing in front of him. In his right hand Ken Jr. held the red toy truck, and in his left hand he held the wheels. Through tears he said, "Daddy, my Christmas is broken already!"

Now, I am happy to report that the red toy truck was fixed pretty quickly. But for me, that episode raises an interesting question: *What are the Christmas gifts that won't break?*

Jesus said something that might help us answer that question. He said, "Do not store up for yourselves treasures on earth, where moth and rust consume and where thieves break in and steal; but store up for yourselves treasures in heaven. . . . For where your treasure is, there your heart will be also" (Matthew 6:19-21). Jesus was giving us a much-needed warning. He was saying, in effect, "Be careful now. Don't get your heart too set on material things. Material things aren't permanent. They wear out, they break, they erode, they go out of fashion, they can be lost or stolen. Material things are nice, but don't get too attached to them. Rather, build your happiness on things you cannot lose, on things that are independent of the chances and the changes of life."

The great poet Robert Burns once wrote a poem about how fleeting things can be and how quickly they can get away from us. He wrote:

> But pleasures are like poppies spread—
> You seize the flower, its bloom is shed;
> Or like the snow falls in the river—
> A moment white, then melts forever.
> ("Tom O'Shanter" [1790])

Any one of us whose life and happiness depend on material things will surely be disappointed, because material things do not last. They go out of style. They wear out. They break.

So during this Advent season, I want us to think together about Christmas gifts that won't break. There are many, of course, but in this four-week season we will focus on the four gifts represented by the four outer candles of the traditional Advent wreath: hope, love, joy, and peace.

It is my prayer that as we go through this four-week Advent season together, we might—as never before—receive from God and then pass on to others the Christmas gifts that won't break

1. The Gift of Hope

Now the birth of Jesus the Messiah took place in this way. When his mother Mary had been engaged to Joseph, but before they lived together, she was found to be with child from the Holy Spirit. Her husband Joseph, being a righteous man and unwilling to expose her to public disgrace, planned to dismiss her quietly. But just when he had resolved to do this, an angel of the Lord appeared to him in a dream and said, "Joseph, son of David, do not be afraid to take Mary as your wife, for the child conceived in her is from the Holy Spirit. She will bear a son, and you are to name him Jesus, for he will save his people from their sins."

MATTHEW 1:18-21

Some years ago our family gathered in Winston-Salem, North Carolina, for the wedding of our nephew. I reserved a room at a local hotel with two double beds, so our daughter Jodi and granddaughter Sarah could share the room with us. Sarah was five years old at the time, and we never knew what she was going to say next.

After the first night at the hotel, I asked Sarah if she had slept well. She said, "Well, Gran, let me explain it like this. At my dayschool we take naps after lunch. But there is a boy in my class named Tyler who snores and I can't get any rest." She paused for a moment, then said, "I think there was a Tyler in our room last night."

Now, according to Matthew 1 there wasn't a Tyler in the room that night with Joseph, but there was an angel, and after his encounter with the angel, Joseph probably didn't get much rest either! Remember the story with me.

Joseph and Mary were engaged and going through the traditional year of betrothal before their formal marriage could take place. They had not had the wedding ceremony yet, were not living together, and had not been physically intimate, but in the eyes of the community they were as good as married. Then, out of the blue, Joseph received word that Mary was expecting! Joseph surely was shaken and heartsick. But he was a kind man and loved Mary, so he decided that instead of publicly humiliating her, he would just break it off quietly.

As Joseph was making his decision, an angel appeared to him in a dream and said words to this effect: "Joseph, don't be afraid. Go ahead and take Mary for your wife. Your love for each other is unique and special. The Spirit is with her bringing a new life. The child is of God. It is God's will that she will bear a son, and you shall call his name Jesus, for he will save his people from their sins."

In the Bible, angels are messengers from God, so imagine the powerful effect of this message of hope. The angel told Joseph not to be afraid and not to abandon Mary, but instead to go ahead and marry her. The angel told Joseph that Mary would give birth to the Savior. And the angel told Joseph to name the baby Jesus. Don't miss this, now: the angel told Joseph what to name the baby!

There are so many remarkable images and lessons in this powerful section of Scripture, but for now let's focus in on the naming of the baby and what it says to us about the gift of hope.

Names Are Important

Have you noticed that people tend to live up—or down—to their names?

I know a man named Smiley. That is his legal name, and it is the ideal name for him because he smiles all the time. Even when he is experiencing life's tough moments, his face has a bright and gracious expression.

I know a man named Happy, and he is one of the happiest people I know.

A woman I know is named Sunny, and the name fits her perfectly. She not only has beautiful blond hair that just glows, but her face is radiant and she has a golden disposition that is warm and wonderful.

I have often wondered, *What if her parents had named her Stormy?* Would she be the same person? Or would she be different?

Then there is John Wesley Dowling, who turned out to be one of the finest Methodists I have ever known.

I'm sure there are exceptions, but more often than not people do indeed live up (or down) to their names. So, parents, be very careful when naming your children! That name can have a dramatic effect on the development of their personalities. Our children may well become what we name them.

The importance of names is a powerful and significant theme in the Bible. *The Interpreter's Dictionary of the Bible* puts it like this: "The giving of personal names in ancient Israel was not merely for the purpose of providing a distinctive label for an individual, but was also commonly [an occasion] for expressing religious convictions associated with the birth of a child or its future" (*Interpreter's Dictionary of the Bible Supplementary Volume* [Nashville: Abingdon Press, 1976], 619).

For example, the name *Elijah* means "the Lord is my God." It's probably no accident that Elijah grew up to be a courageous prophet who called upon his people to worship Yahweh alone and not to bow down to Baal or the other gods of the Canaanite religion.

The name *Moses* was also fitting. It literally means "drawn up out of the water." You probably remember that, as a baby, Moses was saved from being murdered. The Egyptian king, afraid that the Hebrew slaves might grow strong enough to rebel, had ordered for all Hebrew newborn baby boys to be killed. But the family of Moses came up with a creative plan to save his life. They put baby Moses into a basket and placed it among the reeds in the Nile River. The pharaoh's daughter found the baby, "drew him up out of the water," and adopted him. Later, you remember, Moses led the people of Israel through the parted waters of the Red Sea to save them. So Moses was indeed a good name for him.

In the New Testament, one of my favorite characters is Barnabas, whose name means "child of encouragement," which is exactly what he was.

Now, we notice also in the Scriptures that when something dramatic happened to change a person's life, in effect giving them a new birth, their names were often changed to fit their new life. For example, after their covenant with God was made, Abram became Abraham and Sarai became Sarah. After he wrestled with the angel, Jacob became Israel. After his conversion on the Damascus Road, Saul became Paul. And Jesus changed Simon's name to Peter, *Petros,* "the rock."

And that brings us to the passage in Matthew 1.

The Naming of the Christ Child

The angel said to Joseph: "do not be afraid to take Mary as your wife, for the child conceived in her is from the Holy Spirit. She will bear a son, and you are to name him Jesus, for he will save his people from their sins" (Matthew 1:20-21). This announcement is the Christmas hope in a nutshell. It means that God will always be with us—watching over us, reconciling us, and saving us in this world and the world to come.

There is a gospel song that says it like this: "Jesus, Jesus, Jesus . . . There is something about that name." Indeed there is. The name Jesus means "savior" or "the lord's helper." But also notice—don't miss this now—that the name Jesus is the Greek form of the Hebrew name Joshua.

You remember, of course, who Joshua was. As the spiritual tells us, "Joshua fit de battle of Jericho . . . and de walls come tumblin' down." So the name Jesus also means wall-breaker.

Here is how the Apostle Paul expressed it in his letter to the Ephesians, in one of the most powerful statements in all the Bible: "For he is our peace; in his flesh he has made both groups into one and has broken down the dividing wall. . . . So then you are no longer strangers and aliens, but you are citizens with the saints and also members of the household of God, built upon the foundation of the apostles and prophets, with Christ Jesus himself as the cornerstone" (2:14, 19-20).

Now, this idea of Jesus being the wall-breaker, breaking down the dividing walls of hostility, can better be understood when we see it against the backdrop of the Temple's physical layout in the time of Jesus. The Temple was a parable in stone, exposing the prejudices, or walls, that existed in society during biblical times—walls that included a few privileged people but excluded or shut out most. As worshipers moved through the Temple toward the high altar (the Holy of Holies), they encountered a series of walls holding the people back from God.

The first wall held back foreigners, people of other races and nations. The second wall held back women. The third wall held back all men except the priests. The fourth wall, a veil surrounding the Holy of Holies, held back everyone except the High Priest, who was permitted to go inside the veil only once a year, on the Day of Atonement. Even then the other priests tied a rope around his ankle, so that if he fell or passed out, they could pull him back without going inside!

The Holy of Holies, which represented the presence of God, was remote, fearsome, austere, and unapproachable. But then came Jesus, and he broke down the dividing walls and made us one. He brought God out to the people.

When you think of it, that's what Christmas is about: God breaking out, God smashing down the walls, God coming warmly and wonderfully into our lives. And when we forget about Christmas, when we neglect the teachings of Christ, then once again we start building up those walls, fostering hostility and hatred, prejudice and bigotry.

The walls we build today are every bit as real as those in the Temple. Here are some of them:

There are the walls that divide nations. However, Christ came as the Prince of Peace, the Savior of all people, and the Lord of all nations.

There are the walls that divide men and women. The truth is that Christ was the first real liberator of women. Read his teachings, study the Gospels, see how he respected women and included them, and notice how much he advanced the cause of equal rights and equal opportunity.

There are the walls that divide clergy and laity. Jesus made no such distinction. He sent all of the disciples out as ministers.

There are the walls that hold people back from God. More than anything, Jesus brought God to people and people to God. Jesus came not to change God's mind but to reveal it. He came to show us how much God loves us and how available God is to us.

Do you remember what happened in the Temple when Jesus was on the cross? The veil around the Holy of Holies was torn apart, from top to bottom. God did it! God tore it! God broke down that wall!

Jesus Lived Up to His Name

Here is the good news of Christmas: Christ is our Savior, our Redeemer, and our Reconciler. He makes us all one. He breaks down the dividing walls and shows us that we are God's family. And that is our hope for peace on earth and good will toward all people.

This profound truth is captured in a story that was written by an American journalist who spent one Christmas Eve with his family in Paris. He writes that his family's entire trip had been one frustration after another, and they had to settle for a Christmas Eve dinner at a rundown restaurant. There they found a local flower woman who had no customers, German and French families who looked as frustrated as his own, and one American sailor writing a letter home. They had all but lost their Christmas spirit, but then:

> The young sailor finished his meal and got up to leave. Putting on his coat, he walked over to the flower woman's table. "Happy Christmas," he said, smiling and picking out two corsages. . . .
>
> Pressing one of the small corsages flat, he put it into the letter he had written, then handed the woman a twenty franc note.
>
> "I don't have change, monsieur," she said. . . .
>
> "No, ma'am," said the sailor. . . . "This is my Christmas present to you."
>
> Straightening up, he came to our table. . . . "Sir," he said to me, "may I have permission to present these flowers to your beautiful daughter?" In one quick motion he gave my wife the corsage, wished us a merry Christmas, and departed.
>
> Everyone had stopped eating. Everyone had been watching the sailor. Everyone was silent. A few seconds later, Christmas exploded throughout the restaurant like a bomb. The old flower woman jumped up. . . . The piano player began to belt out "Good King Wenceslaus." . . . My wife [sang] . . . and our three sons joined her, bellowing the song with uninhibited enthusiasm.
>
> "Gut! Gut!" shouted the Germans. They jumped on their chairs and began singing the words in German. The waiter embraced the flower woman. Waving their arms, they sang in French. . . .
>
> People crowded in from the street until many customers were standing. . . .
>
> The miserable evening in a shoddy restaurant ended up being the very best Christmas Eve we had ever experienced just because of a young sailor who had Christmas spirit in his soul. He released the love and joy that had been smothered within us by anger and disappointment. He gave us Christmas.
>
> (William J. Lederer, "A Sailor's Christmas Gift," *Chicken Soup for the Christian Soul* [Deerfield Beach, Fla.: HCI, 1997], 320–21)

His name shall be called Jesus the wall-breaker. He will save the people from their sins. Christ is the hope of the world. And hope is a Christmas gift that won't break!

2. The Gift of Love

When the angels had left them and gone into heaven, the shepherds said to one another, "Let us go now to Bethlehem and see this thing that has taken place, which the Lord has made known to us." So they went with haste and found Mary and Joseph, and the child lying in the manger. When they saw this, they made known what had been told them about this child; and all who heard it were amazed at what the shepherds told them. But Mary treasured all these words and pondered them in her heart. The shepherds returned, glorifying and praising God for all they had heard and seen, as it had been told them.

LUKE 2:15-20

Christmas is a time for the telling of stories. Wonderful, heart-warming stories cluster beautifully around Christmas. Here is one of my favorites. Written by M. A. Matthews, it is called "The Gift of a Child."

The day was frightfully cold, . . . with swirls of snow in the air, and I was looking out the living room window . . . which faces our church. Workmen had just finished constructing the annual Nativity scene in the church-yard . . . when school let out for the day. Children gathered excitedly around the crèche, . . . but they didn't stay long; it was far too cold for lingering. All the children took a quick look at the manger scene and then hurried away—except for a tiny girl of about six.

The wind lashed at her bare legs and caused her coat to fly open in the front . . . but she was oblivious of the weather. She was captivated by that manger scene. All her attention was riveted on the statues before her. Which one I couldn't tell. Was it Mary? The baby? The shepherds? The Wise Men? The animals? I wondered!

And then a beautiful and poignant moment. . . . I saw her remove her blue woolen head scarf. The wind quickly knotted her hair into a wild tangle, but she didn't seem to notice that either. She had only one thought. Lovingly, she wrapped her scarf around the statue of the Baby Jesus. After she had covered it, she patted the baby and then kissed Him on the cheek. Satisfied, she skipped on down the street, her hair frosted with tiny diamonds of ice. As I watched that I realized that Christmas had come once again.
(*The Guideposts Christmas Treasury* [New York: Doubleday, 1972], 201)

That touching story raises a question for us to think about together: what is Christmas, and when does it come? Surely Christmas is more than a date on a calendar. Surely Christmas is more than a vague annual nod in the direction of Bethlehem. Surely Christmas is more than poinsettias and presents and parades and pageants, as nice as those are. What puts the meaning of Christmas deep into our souls? What writes the Christmas spirit indelibly on our hearts?

Well, of course, the essence of Christmas is love, God's incredible love for us, expressed when God sent Christ into the world to save us. "Love Came Down at Christmas"—that's how the hymn writer puts it. That's the answer to our question. Whenever and wherever we receive God's sacrificial love, whenever and wherever we pass it on to others, whenever and wherever God's love is accepted and shared, Christmas comes once again!

But how does that happen? Let me bring the answer closer to home with three observations.

When We Love God, There Is Christmas

When we, like the shepherds, fall down in awe, wonder, and commitment before the manger of God's love, there is Christmas! When we, like the three wise men, give our best to the Master, there is Christmas! When we, like Mary and Joseph, trust and obey God and try our best to do God's will, there is Christmas!

A colleague and friend of mine served for many years as a senior minister out West. He tells about an uncomfortable experience he had in a church he served some years ago. In that church, a man had been unusually loud and coarse and boisterous and overbearing, and on many occasions the man had embarrassed the life out of him in public. Every time he saw my friend, the man would shout, "Attention, everybody! Here comes the man of God! Look, everybody, the man of God is here!"

In crowded cafeterias, in busy hotel lobbies, in noisy sports arenas, in congested supermarkets, in quiet libraries, even in elegant restaurants, every time this man saw him he would point dramatically and shout, "Here comes the man of God!"

Now, let me hurry to say that my friend is not ashamed of being a Christian or a minister, but the way the man so blatantly pointed him out was disconcerting. He is a bit shy and reserved, and the man's booming announcement embarrassed him. He said he sort of felt like Clark Kent with his cover blown!

Then one day, after embarrassing my minister friend again, the man spoke directly to him and said, "So how is the man of God today?" "Just fine, thank you," he replied, then asked, "By the way, whose man are you?" The man was silent. He didn't know what to say. He probably didn't like the question very much. Maybe he detected a little irritation in it somewhere. But if we stop to think about it, the question is a good one: By the way, whose man are you? Whose woman are you? Whose child? Whose person? Whose disciple?

One of the best-known and most beloved verses in all the Bible is John 3:16: "For God so loved the world that he gave his only Son, so that everyone who believes in him may not perish but may have eternal life." Listen! That's what Christmas is really all about. We needed a Savior and

God sent us one. We needed a Messiah and God sent us one. We needed a Christ and God sent us one. God so loved the world that he gave the world his only Son.

When we bow down before that, when we come to grips with that, when we accept God's love, when we receive the Messiah into our hearts and commit our lives in faith to him, whenever and wherever that happens, there is Christmas. Whenever and wherever that happens, Christmas comes once again.

When We Love Our Families, There Is Christmas

From that very first silent and holy night long ago in Bethlehem, Christmas has been a family matter. Just as the shepherds were drawn to the stable, even so at Christmas today we are drawn toward home. We feel a longing to go home for Christmas, to be with our families. Unfortunately, in many homes this Christmas there will be a chill in the air. You see, there is a big difference between everybody being at home . . . and being at home with everybody.

Sadly, in some families there is estrangement, alienation, division, uneasiness, tension, bitterness, hostility, made all the more graphic by the sacredness of the Christmas season. And that is so pathetic, so sad, so tragic to me. How many squabbles will break out this Christmas because somebody in a family got mad? How many obscenities will be screamed? How many embarrassing scenes will unfold? How many people will be injured or killed because some family members can't get along this Christmas?

A few years ago, a young college student came to see me. It was just a few days after Christmas, and I could tell immediately that she was happy. Her face was radiant, glowing with joy. "We had the best Christmas ever," she told me. I answered, "Oh, you got some nice presents, did you?" "Well," she said, "I did get some wonderful gifts, but that wasn't what made it special." She paused for a moment, then said, "Jim, I'm twenty years old now. And for the first time in my twenty years, Mom and Dad didn't get into a big fight at Christmas! It was the best Christmas we ever had!"

Whenever and wherever there is peace and harmony and tenderness and respect and thoughtfulness and caring in the family, Christmas comes once again. When we love God, and when we love our families, there is Christmas!

When We Love Other People, There Is Christmas

Many years ago, there lived in a small village a cobbler by the name of Conrad. Day by day, early and late, the tap, tap, tap of his hammer could be heard as he mended the shoes brought to him by the villagers. Though alone and poor, this kindly older man always had a warm and friendly word for everyone. As a result, many folks took lighter hearts away from his hut, along with their carefully mended shoes.

Now, Christmas is a time when families draw close together, but Conrad had no family with whom he could share his Christmas. On Christmas morning, some neighbors, thinking how lonely Conrad must feel, decided to pay him a visit. They found him sweeping away the snow in front of his home, and to their surprise his face was radiant and happy as he greeted them.

As they entered his house, they gazed in amazement. Instead of a dreary room, they saw a place made festive with holly and evergreen. Christmas decorations brightened the walls and hung gracefully from the rafters. And the table was set for two. Obviously, Conrad was expecting a guest. "Who is coming to visit you?" the neighbors asked. Conrad replied, "Last night the Lord appeared to me in a dream. He told me that I would not be alone on Christmas Day, for he himself was coming to be my guest. That is why I have prepared so joyfully. Everything is ready now. I am waiting for him to come."

After the neighbors left, Conrad sat by the window, quietly watching and waiting for the Lord to come. As he watched, the minutes passed into hours, but he scarcely noticed because he was so excited. While he watched, a beggar passed his window, ragged, weary, almost frozen in the harsh winter winds. Conrad called him in. He offered the beggar the warmth of his humble home and gave him some shoes for his frozen feet.

After the beggar left, an old woman hobbled by, carrying on her back a heavy load of firewood. Conrad ran out, lifted the load from her back, and helped her into his little home. There he gave her some food for her starved body, and after she had rested a bit he helped the woman on her way.

Once again Conrad positioned himself by the window to watch for his Lord. This time he heard the sound of a child sobbing. Conrad opened his front door and found a little girl wandering lost and frightened in the snow. Some warm milk and soothing words stilled the frightened cries, and soon afterward Conrad restored the lost child to her mother's arms. Once more Conrad returned to his vigil. But now the sun was sinking, and the wintry Christmas day was coming to an end.

But where was his promised guest? Anxious and weary and somewhat disappointed, Conrad dropped to his knees and prayed, "Oh, Lord, where were you? I waited and watched for you all day. Why didn't you come?"

Out of the silence came a voice: "Oh, Conrad, my Conrad, don't be dismayed. This very day, three times I came to your door. Three times my shadow crossed your floor. I was the beggar with frozen feet. I was the woman you fed. I was a little girl who was lost."

The message of this story is a big part of Christmas: "Truly I tell you, just as you did it to one of the least of these who are members of my family, you did it to me." When we see Christ in other people and love them, then at that precise moment Christmas comes once again.

When we love God, when we love our families, when we love other people, there is Christmas. The Christmas gift of love is surely a Christmas gift that won't break!

3. The Gift of Joy

All this took place to fulfill what had been spoken by the Lord through the prophet: "Look, the virgin shall conceive and bear a son, and they shall name him Emmanuel," which means, "God is with us." When Joseph awoke from sleep, he did as the angel of the Lord commanded him; he took her as his wife, but had no marital relations with her until she had borne a son; and he named him Jesus.

MATTHEW 1:22-25

A young mother wanted her two preschool-aged children to learn the real meaning of Christmas, so early that December she brought home a small manger scene. The figurines in the manger scene were made of wood, so they were pretty much indestructible—and easy for little hands to pick up and move around.

The children loved the manger scene, and they loved being able to arrange and rearrange the figurines in creative and childlike ways. As you might imagine, sometimes the figurines would disappear and later show up in the most fascinating places around the house.

Interestingly, the character that most often disappeared was Jesus. The mother would walk by and see that Jesus was missing again. Once she found him on the windowsill in her daughter's room. How appropriate, thought the mother: Jesus was born in a stable, but he moved out of the manger to go with us and watch over us wherever we may go.

A few days before Christmas, the Jesus figurine disappeared again. The mother looked all over the house and could not find him anywhere. When time came to put the manger scene away, Jesus was still missing. She called the children to the manger scene and asked, "Where is Jesus?" Her five-year-old daughter scrunched up her shoulders and stuck out her hands, palms upward, in that universal gesture that means "Search me. I don't know. I have no idea. I don't have a clue."

The mother then turned to her two-year-old son and asked, "Do you know where Jesus is?" Her son became very animated and began talking a mile a minute. But, as is sometimes the case with two-year-olds, it sounded like gibberish. The boy knew what he was saying, but his mother and sister couldn't understand it.

Finally the boy went over, took his mother by the hand, and led her to his room. He pointed to his bed. The mother pulled back the covers and looked, with no luck. Then the boy pointed to his pillow. Finally she found the Jesus figurine—under her son's pillow!

Isn't that beautiful? You see, for many two-year-olds, bedtime is scary time. It's dark in the room, and they feel all alone. But this young boy felt safe and secure because Jesus was there with him!

That's the good news of Christmas, isn't it? We find that incredible truth expressed with these magnificent words in the first chapter of Matthew: "They shall name him Emmanuel, which means, 'God is with us.' "

Here is the great truth of Christmas, the great message of Christmas, the great promise of Christmas, the great joy of Christmas, all wrapped up in that one word, Emmanuel, which means God is always with us!

The good news of Christmas gives us a deep sense of hope, of love, and of joy. Let me show you what I mean.

The Joy of Encouragement

In this world, people get criticized too much, "put down" too much, and "fussed at" too much, so we in the church (who are the children of Christmas) need to be the sons and daughters of encouragement. The message of Christmas is good news, glad tidings, great joy. Christ came to lift people up, not tear them down. Christ came to save people, not destroy them. We would do well to pick up his torch and take on his spirit of joyful encouragement.

Have you heard about the little boy who was in the school Christmas play? He was playing the part of an angel. He was to come to the shepherds in the field and announce Christ's birth with enthusiasm and excitement. But he was having real trouble learning his part. He was especially finding it difficult to say his line, "Behold, I bring you glad tidings of great joy." The boy didn't normally talk that way, so he found the line hard to memorize. The drama teacher worked with him and explained that "glad tidings" simply meant good news. Finally, the boy learned his part. But on the night of the play, the boy got stage fright and forgot his line. Instead of saying, "Behold, I bring you glad tidings of great joy," the little angel made this Christmas play different from any other by suddenly running all over the stage, flapping his wings wildly, and shouting over and over, "Boy, have I got good news for you!"

That's part of our task as Christians, isn't it? We need to say to a scared, anxious, confused, fretful world, "Boy, have we got good news for you!" The good news is that we can make it because God is with us and will see us through. Our part of that good news is saying to people near us, "I care about you," "I believe in you," "I trust you," "You can do it."

Maybe the best gift we can give someone we love this Christmas is a gift that will not break: the joy of encouragement.

The Joy of Thoughtfulness

One of the things I love most about Christmas is the way it brings out people's thoughtfulness. Christmas cards, gifts, flowers, food, phone calls, e-mails—these wonderful gestures of thoughtfulness are woven deeply into the fabric of Christmas.

A few years ago, when I was on the staff of the First United Methodist Church in Shreveport, Louisiana, some members of our outreach committee came to me a few days before Christmas with a concern and a plan. They were concerned that some people in our community might be hungry or lonely on Christmas Day. Their plan was to open our church fellowship hall on Christmas afternoon and offer free food and warm fellowship—a Christmas party—to anyone who might be hungry or lonely. I asked them if they would be willing to give up their Christmas afternoon to work in the kitchen. They said they would be glad to and that they had already recruited several others to help. So we announced to the city that anyone who might be hungry or lonely on Christmas afternoon could come to the church between noon and five o'clock to enjoy Christmas carols, fellowship, and a complimentary meal.

Just after lunch on Christmas afternoon, I drove to the church to see how things were going. It was about two o'clock when I got there. As I went inside, I met several members of our outreach committee coming out the door and heading for home. "What happened?" I asked. "Is it over? Didn't anybody show up?" A committee member answered, "Oh, they are in there for sure. About three hundred are eating right now. The only reason we are leaving is that some new workers came in to relieve us." I asked, "Who?" The committee member smiled and said, "Why don't you go into the kitchen and see for yourself?"

When I went into the kitchen, I was moved to tears by what I saw: There was my good friend, a rabbi, along with fourteen members of his temple, who had told our people, "This is your special day. Go home and be with your families, and we will work for you."

Isn't that something? One of the most moving Christmas gifts I ever saw came from a group of Jewish friends who had heard what we were trying to do and had responded with joy—the joy of thoughtfulness.

The Joy of Graciousness

The joy of gracious, sacrificial love—that's what it's all about, isn't it?

Glenn Kittler writes of a Franciscan priest named Father Bonaventure, who gave a Christmas party for some Native American children of the Papago tribe near Tucson, Arizona. It was their first Christmas party. There were games and races, with prizes for the winners. One little boy named Luis Pablo was especially excited to be there. He told Father Bonaventure that he needed to win three prizes. Luis tried hard. He entered every game and ran in every race but, much to his dismay, did not win a single prize. At the end of the party, the children formed a line, and to each of them Father Bonaventure presented a bag of hard candy. When eight-year-old Luis Pablo received his, he asked for three more. Father Bonaventure refused him sternly.

However, Luis explained he only wanted *empty* bags, so Father Bonaventure shrugged and thought, *Why not?* He gave Luis three bags, and the boy left, smiling. Later, the priest looked out the window and saw Luis sitting with the three bags open beside him, carefully dividing his candy into the bags. Father Bonaventure suddenly remembered that Luis had two little brothers and a sister at home who were too young to come to the party. Going into the party room, Father Bonaventure collected all the remaining candy into a large bag, went outside, and gave it to Luis.

"Here's your prize," he said.
"Prize?" Luis asked, suspicious. "What for?"

"All during the party I was watching to see which one of you had the true spirit of Christmas . . . you win."
(*The Guideposts Christmas Treasury* [New York: Doubleday, 1972], 206)

The essence of Christmas is the joy of gracious, sacrificial love. Christ came to show us what God is like and what God wants us to be like, and the word is *love*: love came down at Christmas, and the joy it brings is the best and most unbreakable gift of all!

4. The Gift of Peace

In that region there were shepherds living in the fields, keeping watch over their flock by night. Then an angel of the Lord stood before them, and the glory of the Lord shone around them, and they were terrified. But the angel said to them, "Do not be afraid; for see—I am bringing you good news of great joy for all the people: to you is born this day in the city of David a Savior, who is the Messiah, the Lord. This will be a sign for you: you will find a child wrapped in bands of cloth and lying in a manger." And suddenly there was with the angel a multitude of the heavenly host, praising God and saying, "Glory to God in the highest heaven, and on earth peace among those whom he favors!"

LUKE 2:8-14

A beautiful old Christmas legend tells of how God called the angels of heaven together one day for a special choir rehearsal. God told them of a special song they were to learn, a song they would sing at a very significant occasion. So the angels went to work on it. They rehearsed long and hard, with great focus and intensity. In fact, some of the angels grumbled a bit, but God insisted on a very high standard for the choir.

As time passed, the choir improved in tone, in rhythm, and in quality. Finally God announced that they were ready, but then God shocked them a bit. God told them that they would sing the song only once, and only on one night. There would be just one performance. Again, some of the angels grumbled. The song was so extraordinarily beautiful, and they had it down pat now. Surely they could sing it many times. God just smiled and told them that when the time came, they would understand.

Finally one night, God called the choir together. The angels gathered above a field just outside of Bethlehem. "It's time," God told them, and the angels sang their song. Oh, my, did they sing it! "Glory to God in the highest, and on earth peace and good will toward all." And as the angels sang, they knew there would never be another night like this one, and that there would never be another birth like this birth in Bethlehem.

When the angels returned to heaven, God reminded them that they could hum the song occasionally as individuals if they wanted to, but they would not sing it again formally as an angelic choir. One angel was bold enough to step forward and ask God why not. They had performed it so beautifully. It had felt so right. Why couldn't they sing that great song anymore?

God smiled. "Because," God said, "my son has been born, and now earth must do the singing!"

Once each year, Christmas comes around again to remind us of what God said: that God's Son has come to earth, and now we must do the singing! And look at how we have tried. Without question, one of the best and most beloved parts of the Christmas celebration is the music. The good news of Christmas is so awesome, so full of wonder, that it's not enough just to talk about it. We have to burst forth in song. We have to sing it.

Think of it! There are the traditional anthems of Handel, Beethoven, Mozart, and Bach, as well as the powerful modern works of Rutter, Davis, and Landes. There are beloved carols such as "O Little Town of Bethlehem," "Joy to the World," "The First Noel," "Silent Night," and "O

Come, All Ye Faithful." And there are popular songs such as "Jingle Bells," "Winter Wonderland," and "I'll Be Home for Christmas."

Recently I was in a department store doing some Christmas shopping. Christmas music was playing, and I was getting into the spirit of it all, when suddenly I realized that I was singing along with Vince Gill. Vince and I were performing the hymn "Let There Be Peace on Earth and Let It Begin with Me." Vince and I were sounding pretty good, mainly because Vince can sing and because it is a great Christmas hymn (as well as a great hymn for all seasons), with a beautiful melody and an even more beautiful life-lesson in it.

The words of that hymn are a big part of the Christmas message: God loves us and claims us as beloved children, and God wants us to live in the spirit of peaceful unity and harmony as sisters and brothers in God's family. In fact, God wants us to live each day in the spirit of peacemakers. Look at those words again: "Let there be peace on earth and let it begin with me." Let it start with me. Let me live every day as a peacemaker—in other words, in the gracious spirit of Jesus Christ.

That's the way it works. Christmas is the dramatic reminder that Christ came into this world to redeem us and to bring peace to our troubled souls. If in faith we will accept it, Christmas has a great gift for us: the gift of peace. Christmas offers us peace with God, peace with ourselves, and peace with others.

Peace with God

Jesus Christ came into this world to set us right with God. Jesus Christ came into the world to save us and to bring us back to God. It's what Christmas is all about.

You may have heard the old story about the elderly couple driving down the street one day. It was Christmastime, and the husband was driving. As they listened to the beautiful music of Christmas on the radio, the wife became nostalgic and said, "Herbert, do you remember how we used to sit so close together as we drove along? It was so wonderful back then. What happened?" Herbert replied, "I don't know about that. All I know is that I haven't moved."

Well, Christmas comes each year to remind us that God is not the one who has moved away from us. No! We are the ones who have moved. We are the ones who have drifted away from God.

Some years ago, a friend told me a story about taking his five-year-old son Christmas shopping one Saturday morning. It was just a day or so before Christmas, and the department store was packed with shoppers. He told his son to stay near him and not wander off, because he could get lost in the crowd. After they had shopped together for a while, he was buying something for his wife at one of the counters. When he completed the purchase, he looked back and his son was not there. He frantically searched for his son. He called out to him and rushed through the crowd looking for him, with no success. He checked the candy counter and then the toy department. Surely his son would be there! But no, his son wasn't anywhere to be found.

Just as he was starting to panic, there was an announcement over the loudspeaker: "We have a lost boy here! If you have lost your little boy, please come to the service desk." He anxiously made his way to the desk, and sure enough, there was his lost child. It was a big reunion, with lots of hugs and words of love and more visits to the candy counter and the toy department. They had been apart, but they had found each other again! They had been brought back together.

Now, think about this. The two of them had been separated because the little boy had wandered off, and it was the person who spoke over the loudspeaker who got them back together again. That person served, in a sense, as a reconciler between a father and his little boy.

In the same sense, Christ came to this earth to help us get back together with God, who made us and who loves us. That's what the word

Emmanuel means: God is with us. God comes in the Christ Child to seek and save the lost. That's what Christmas is all about. That's the way we can have the peace of Christmas: to let the Christ of Christmas bring us back to the Father who loves us.

Peace with Ourselves

More and more psychologists are telling us that we can't feel good about life and other people until we feel good about ourselves. They call it a healthy self-esteem, which is simply another way of saying that we need to be right with ourselves.

Have you heard about the man who wrote a letter to the Internal Revenue Service? The letter said, "Dear sirs: I underpaid my tax bill for last year. I can't sleep at night and my conscience is bothering me. Enclosed please find $600." He then added a P.S.: "If I still can't sleep, I'll send the rest."

I recently saw a fascinating movie about the famous golfer Bobby Jones. Called *Stroke of Genius*, the movie takes us back to a time when Jones was the talk of the golfing world. Bobby Jones was born on March 17, 1902, in Atlanta, Georgia. He was a child prodigy in golf, winning his first tournament at the age of six. By the time he was twelve, he was the Georgia state golf champion, and in 1921, at age nineteen, he became the youngest member of the U.S. Walker Cup team when it journeyed to England. Between 1923 and 1930, Jones won five U.S. amateur titles, four U.S. Opens, three British Opens, and one British amateur title. In 1930 he achieved the "Grand Slam," winning all four of the major golf tournaments in a single calendar year, the only golfer in history ever to accomplish that feat. Amazingly, Jones retired from golf at the young age of twenty-eight. He became a lawyer and in 1934 he helped design the Augusta National Golf Club, where he founded the noted Masters Golf Tournament.

But with all his incredible accomplishments as a golf champion, Bobby Jones may be even more well-known and respected for a tournament he didn't win! It was the U.S. Open, and *Stroke of Genius* depicts the scene powerfully. Jones hits his ball into the rough. As he stands over the ball for his second shot, his ball moves slightly. No one else sees this, but Jones immediately tells an official that he caused his ball to move. The officials huddle up and discuss the situation. Then they come back to Jones and tell him, "Bobby, we've talked to your opponent, to all the officials, and to several people in the gallery, and nobody saw your ball move. It's your call. Are you sure you caused that ball to move?" Jones answers, "I know I did." The lead official looks at him and says, "Son, you are to be congratulated!" To which Jones says, "Sir, that is like congratulating me for not robbing a bank. I don't know how else to play the game." It was a two-stroke penalty, and (can you believe it?) Bobby Jones lost that U.S. Open tournament by one stroke!

What he did that day prompted noted sportswriter O. B. Keeler to write these words: "Bobby Jones lost the U.S. Open today by one stroke. In calling a penalty on himself, he demonstrated for all of us the highest ideals of sportsmanship and personal honor. I am prouder of him than if he had won." Bobby Jones said of his actions, "There are things finer than winning championships." Today, appropriately, the United States Golf Association's sportsmanship prize is named the Bobby Jones Award.

Let me ask you something. Do you feel good about your life right now? About who you are and what you've done? No matter how we feel, we can find peace with ourselves by welcoming the Prince of Peace into our hearts and lives. The only way we can be right with ourselves is to be made right by him.

Peace with Others

A friend of mine, in her eighties and full of life, has a very special Christmas headband. It has mistletoe above it on a spring. When she wears it, she is under the mistletoe no matter where she goes! Two weeks before Christmas every year, she puts on her headband and wears it everywhere, spreading Christmas joy with her beautiful radiance and her wonderful sense of humor. She is delightful! And she gets lots of kisses and hugs and smiles.

Do you know where the custom of kissing under the mistletoe came from? It began with the druids in northern Europe. They believed mistletoe had curative powers and could heal lots of things, including separation between people. So when two enemies happened to meet under an oak tree with mistletoe hanging above them, they took it as a sign from God that they should drop their weapons and be reconciled. They would set aside their animosities and embrace each other under the mistletoe.

When Christian missionaries moved into northern Europe, they saw this mistletoe custom as a perfect symbol for what happened at Christmas—that Jesus Christ came into the world to save us, to redeem us, and to bring us peace, healing, forgiveness, love, and reconciliation. He came to show us God's love and to show us how to love one another. In a real sense, the Prince of Peace came to show us how to embrace one another, as the druids did, and live together in peace.

If you want to have a "peace-full" Christmas, go in the spirit of love and fix the broken relationships in your life. If you are alienated or estranged or cut off or at odds with any other person, go in the spirit of Christmas and make peace. Don't put it off any longer. Drop your pride, your resentment, your grudges, and go set it right. With the help of God, go make peace today. Christmas offers us the gift of peace with others, but it's up to us to accept that gift.

At Christmas, the Christ Child comes into the world as the Prince of Peace. He brings the peace that passes understanding, the peace that we are called to pass on to others.

Hope. Love. Joy. And Peace.

These are the Christmas gifts that always fit.

These are the Christmas gifts that never go out of style.

These are the Christmas gifts wrapped in heaven.

These are the Christmas gifts that we as Christian disciples are called upon to pass on to others.

These are the Christmas gifts that won't break!

Study Guide

*C*hristmas Gifts That Won't Break: An Advent Study for Adults is a book that can be used in a small-group experience designed to help participants enrich their celebration of the Christmas season. This adult study is part of a multi-age experience that includes two companion studies:

James W. Moore's
Christmas Gifts That Won't Break:
An Advent Study for Children

James W. Moore's
Christmas Gifts That Won't Break:
An Advent Study for Youth

Together, these three studies give your church everything needed to create a churchwide Advent series for the whole family. In addition to activities for each age level, you'll find suggestions for an all-church event that makes use of the three studies. These suggestions are presented in the section following this study guide.

As a discussion leader for the adult study, you will have the opportunity to help those in your group grow closer to God through this experience. Together over each of four sessions, your group will read and discuss a lesson and share insights about Advent based on the session theme. This study guide provides discussion questions for each session, along with a prayer and focus for the week.

The format is simple. Encourage participants to read the material for each session before the group meeting; alternatively, if time allows, they can read the material as a group at the session. Then, after reading, participants will react to and interact with questions provided in this study guide for you, the group leader. The questions are designed to stimulate discussion and help group members receive new insights about Advent. As group leader, your job will be to begin and to moderate the discussion.

Here are some thoughts on how to best facilitate this process:

- Your small group will meet four times to discuss the four Advent themes. Each meeting will last 45 to 90 minutes. As leader, you can adjust the number and depth of questions to fit the time allotted for the meeting.
- Be sure everyone knows the time and place of each meeting. Meetings may be held at church or in the homes of group members.
- Leading is easy. As group leader, you simply facilitate the discussion that will follow the reading of the lesson. The format is the same for each meeting: reading aloud the scripture and then each of the six discussion questions. You may conclude with a prayer, read by you or a group member, and ask group members to observe the focus for the week.
- Prior to the meeting, familiarize yourself with the material. Read the lesson and the discussion questions.
- Select the discussion questions from this study guide that you believe are best suited to your group. Remember, you do not have to use all the questions, and you can create your own questions and activities.

- Encourage group members to participate as they feel comfortable doing so.

- As group leader, do whatever you can to make group members feel welcome to voice their ideas, opinions, and insights.

- Encourage questions. Remind participants that all questions are valid as part of the learning process. By asking questions, you give permission for people to share with others, exchanging thoughts and feelings.

- Model a style of openness, honesty, and warmth. Don't ask group members to share anything they are uncomfortable discussing. At times, consider being the first to share, particularly when talking about personal experiences.

- Some questions may be more difficult to answer than others. If you ask a question and no one responds, begin the discussion by venturing an answer yourself. Then ask for comments and other answers. Remember that most questions have multiple answers.

- Ask the follow-up question "Why?" or "Why do you believe that?" to help continue a discussion and give it greater depth.

- Give everyone a chance to talk, but keep the conversation moving. Occasionally you may want to direct a question gently to people in the group who have been quiet. Remember to keep the sharing focused on faith and personal experiences. Moderate the discussion to prevent a few individuals from doing all the talking.

- Remember that as a leader you do not have to know all the answers. Also remember that questions of faith are often a matter of opinion and there may be differing opinions within the group. Your job is to keep the discussion moving and to encourage participation.

- One way to conclude the discussion is by asking a general question such as "How has this discussion helped or challenged you?" Before ending the discussion, be sure to ask group members if they have any questions that have not been answered.

- Honor the time schedule. Allow the meeting to run longer than planned only if the group agrees to the extra time.
- Be grateful and supportive. Thank people for their ideas and their participation.

Remember, you are not expected to be a "perfect" leader. You are expected to do the best you can by focusing on the participants and the session.

1. The Gift of Hope

Discussion Questions

1. What does Advent mean to you? Why is it important? What do you hope to receive from participating in this small-group experience?

2. Discuss the encounter of Joseph and the angel. What feelings do you think Joseph experienced?

3. Why are names important? Discuss some of the ways in which names are chosen. Describe how and why you received your name.

4. List and discuss the meanings of the name *Jesus*. Why do you think this name is appropriate?

5. In what ways could Jesus have been considered a wall-breaker during his ministry?

6. In what ways does Jesus represent the gift of hope?

Prayer

Dear God, thank you for the season of Advent and the gift of hope. Help us prepare our hearts for your coming and to remember the true meaning of Christmas. Amen.

Focus for the Week

Begin your observance of Advent by becoming an instrument of hope to others this week. Give the gift of hope to those who need it by giving of yourself. As Christmas draws near, look for opportunities to become a messenger of good news.

2. The Gift of Love

Discussion Questions

1. Describe a time when you experienced the gift of love. How did it make you feel? How did you respond?

2. What connections do you see between John 3:16 and the Christmas season?

3. List some of the many ways that love of family can be shown. What are some examples from your own experience?

4. What are some ways in which the act of loving other people brings about and enhances Christmas?

5. Why is love the perfect gift? List some of the many reasons this gift is cherished.

6. What are some ways we can show our love for God at Christmas?

Prayer

Dear God, thank you for the gift of love. May we share this gift with others and learn how to love unconditionally. Help us during this Christmas season to practice love in action with family, friends, and strangers. Amen.

Focus for the Week

This week, consider ways to express your love of other people. Take some risks in doing so with family and friends. Practice acts of love and kindness toward strangers. Respond to others as Jesus would do, in compassion and with a willingness to meet human needs.

3. The Gift of Joy

Discussion Questions

1. Name some times in life when we experience joy. What are some examples from your own life?

2. The name *Emmanuel* means "God is with us." What are some reasons that this is so?

3. What does "joyful encouragement" mean to you? What are some examples from your own life?

4. In your experience, does Christmas bring out thoughtfulness in people? Why do you think this is?

5. What are some ways in which we experience the joy of graciousness at Christmas?

6. When you think of the Christmas gift of joy, what thoughts or images come to mind?

Prayer

Dear God, thank you for the gift of joy and for the way it brightens our days. Help us give joy to others through what we say and do. Show us how to make this Christmas a true season of joy. Amen.

Focus for the Week

Practice being a joyful person this week. Give joy to others. Look for opportunities to open the eyes of others to the joys of the season. Count your blessings and the many joys of your life.

4. The Gift of Peace

Discussion Questions

1. Think of times in your life when you needed the gift of peace. Did you receive it? Why or why not?

2. What does it means to be a peacemaker and to give the gift of peace?

3. During the Christmas season, what are some of the ways in which we receive the gift of peace?

4. What are some of the ways in which we can seek inner peace? Recall and share some of the times when you successfully found inner peace.

5. What factors can prevent us from being at peace with others? List some simple ways to become a more peaceful person.

6. How has this Advent study helped you prepare for Christmas?

Prayer

Dear God, thank you for the gift of peace. Help us put peace into practice in our lives and show others the path to true peace. Remind us to serve as peacemakers and to share the love of God with those in need. Amen.

Focus for the Week

Christmas will be here soon. Focus this week on the spirit of the season. Spread gifts of hope, love, joy, and peace to those in need of lasting gifts. Prepare your heart for Christmas and find ways to help others do the same. Live in peace as Christmas draws near.

Suggestions for
an All-Church Event

*C*hristmas Gifts That Won't Break encourages people to experience God's gifts of hope, love, joy, and peace during the Advent season. These gifts never break! Author James W. Moore reminds us that material things wear out, break, erode, go out of fashion, and can be lost or stolen. He invites us to build our happiness on things we cannot lose.

A churchwide Advent program for all ages will help people learn more about the unbreakable gifts God offers through the birth of Jesus, gifts that give us more abundant life. It will offer opportunities for learning, for intergenerational projects and activities, and for reaching out to the community with hope, joy, love, and peace. The following resources are available:

James W. Moore's
Christmas Gifts That Won't Break:
An Advent Study for Adults

James W. Moore's
Christmas Gifts That Won't Break:
An Advent Study for Youth

James W. Moore's
Christmas Gifts That Won't Break:
An Advent Study for Children

Schedule

Many churches have **weeknight programs** that include an evening meal, an intergenerational gathering time, and classes for children, youth, and adults. The following schedule illustrates one way to organize a weeknight program.

5:30 p.m.	Meal
6:00 p.m.	Intergenerational gathering introducing Advent gifts and the lighting of an Advent candle. The time may include presentations, skits, music, and opening or closing prayers.
6:15-8:45 p.m.	Classes for children, youth, and adults

Churches may want to do the Advent study as a **Sunday school** program. This setting would be similar to the weeknight setting. The following schedule takes into account a shorter class time, which is the norm for Sunday morning programs.

10 minutes	Intergenerational gathering
45 minutes	Classes for Children, youth, and adults

Choose a schedule that works best for your congregation and its existing Christian education programs.

Activity Suggestions

All-Church Missions Baby Shower
Ask participants to bring new baby items to give to a homeless shelter, battered women's shelter, or food pantry. End the mission project with a party. Snacks and games can be found in the children's study.

Family Advent Wreaths
Directions for making simple Advent wreaths can be found in Lesson One of the children's study.

Advent Candle Lighting
You may choose to use the prayers below (also found in the adult study guide) as part of lighting the Advent candle during worship.

First Sunday of Advent: The Gift of Hope
Leader: "The unbreakable gift for this first Sunday of Advent is the gift of hope."
Light the first candle.
Pray: Dear God, thank you for the season of Advent and the gift of hope. Help us to prepare our hearts for your coming and to re-member the true meaning of Christmas. Amen.

Second Sunday of Advent: The Gift of Love
Leader: "The unbreakable gift for this second Sunday of Advent is the gift of love."
Light two candles.
Pray: Dear God, thank you for the gift of love. May we share this gift with others and learn how to love unconditionally. Help us practice love in action with family, friends, and strangers during this Christmas season. Amen.

Third Sunday of Advent: The Gift of Joy

Leader: "The unbreakable gift for this third Sunday of Advent is the gift of joy."

Light three candles.

Pray: Dear God, thank you for the gift of joy and for the way it brightens our days. Help us give joy to others through what we say and do. Show us how to make this Christmas a true season of joy. Amen.

Fourth Sunday of Advent: The Gift of Peace

Leader: "The unbreakable gift for this fourth Sunday of Advent is the gift of peace."

Light four candles.

Pray: Dear God, thank you for the gift of peace. Help us put peace into practice in our lives and show others the path to true peace. Remind us to serve as peacemakers and to share the love of God with those in need. Amen.